# EASY TO MAKE

## PARTY AND TABLE DECORATIONS

Juliet Moxley

BROCKHAMPTON PRESS
LONDON

Dedication
For the late Violet Walters, a true friend.

First published in Great Britain in 1993
by Anaya Publishers Ltd, Strode House,
44-50 Osnaburgh Street, London NW1 3ND

This edition published 1995 by Brockhampton Press,
a member of Hodder Headline PLC Group

**Editor** Eve Harlow
**Design** by Design 23
**Photography** Steve Tanner
**Stylist** Katherine Yeates
**Artwork and illustrations** Kate Simunek

British Library Cataloguing in Publication Data
Moxley, Juliet
Easy to Make Party and Table Decorations
(Easy to Make Series)
I. Title   II. Series
ISBN 1-86019-199-1

Typeset by Servis Filmsetting Ltd, Manchester, UK
Colour reproduction by Scantrans Pte Ltd, Singapore
Printed and bound in EC

# CONTENTS

# Introduction

*Everyone loves a celebration, whether it be a dinner party for twelve, a children's birthday party or just a few friends gathering together to celebrate an anniversary.*

Arranging your home to welcome guests is part of being a good host or hostess. The amount of money you spend is often immaterial: the warmth of the welcome and the atmosphere you have created for them instantly makes guests feel at their best. Everyone begins to enjoy themselves, as soon as they step through the door. Then, if you are serving a meal and you have been innovative with your theme, the effect of your table generates excitement. The lighting, subdued and flattering, the sparkle of crystal and silver, the crisp napery and soft elegance of flowers, all these contribute to your guests' enjoyment of the occasion. Planning the decorative effect of a party is as much an art as choosing the right food and wine – and just as important.

But dinner parties are not the only kind of celebrations we decorate our homes for. There are the more casual occasions, when you want to create an atmosphere of fun and jollity. There are outdoor parties, where there may be a certain formality, but where your party decorations can be frivolous and pretty. And, of course, there are parties for children and teenagers where the decorative theme is all-important – and the food sometimes takes second place!

**About this book**

Many of the decorations in this book are made on a budget, from bits and pieces that you already have around your home.

For quick and easy reference, I have divided the book into sections. The first chapter is on centrepieces, something to decorate the centre of your party table. In this chapter, there is a simple, frosted fruit arrangement, which anyone can do, an unusual bowl made of ice, a fabulous

bandbox for a children's party and, not least, a way to create a bowl of glittering, gold-painted fruit, plus some easy-to-make paper poppies. Nothing very difficult, or expensive here!

## Every kind of party

In the chapter devoted to room decoration, I have shown you how to swag a table for a wedding or Christening party, using muslin and flowers, the how-to for making fascinating, floating rose candles and an original idea of mine for using pine-cones – a tree-shaped wall ornament. There are some Hallowe'en party cut-outs for young people to make in this chapter plus an insight in salt dough modelling – a popular and inexpensive craft for people of every age.

The table setting chapter has dozens of ideas for you, for Easter parties, for Christenings and weddings, for national holiday celebrations and children's parties – and ideas for stunning after-dark outdoor parties.

Almost every hostess I know is on the look-out for a new idea in napkin folding so I have included several interesting styles for you to try. Place cards, too, can help to set the mood for a party table and in this chapter I have suggested several ways that you can make these, to fit in with a theme.

## And, of course, there is Christmas

The one time of year when party decorating comes into its own is at Christmas, so I make no excuse for including several Christmas projects in this book. It is one of my most favourite times for entertaining family and friends and I could have filled a book three times over with ideas for decking the hall!

The final chapter is called Better techniques and this is full of advice, helpful hints – and more ideas for party giving. There is a section on making ribbon bows, professional tips on handling flowers and greenery, advice on working with card, paper and adhesives – and much, much more.

So, use this book as a starting-off point to organising better and better parties for your friends and family. Every project has been tested – and they work – and from my designs you are sure to devise other ideas and schemes of your own.

I had a lot of fun in planning the book. I hope you will find it useful in creating many wonderful and successful celebrations.

# ONE

# Centrepieces

# Frosted fruit

*The amount of effort involved in making this decorative centrepiece belies its sophisticated look. It is very easy – all you need are fruits, sugar and egg-white.*

## Materials
Fresh but firm fruits, without bruises or
  broken places, any of the following:
  lemons, oranges, peaches, pears,
  plums, apricots, apples, grapes,
  strawberries
Granulated sugar in a sifter
Egg-white, lightly beaten
Green leaves
Gold or silver doily

## Preparation
1 Wipe all the fruits. Arrange the leaves
round the edges of a glass cake stand.
Place the doily on the leaves.

## Working the design
2 Hold one of the larger pieces of fruit
by its stalk and brush with egg-white,
using a pastry brush.

Hold the prepared fruit by its stalk and sift sugar over it.

3 Hold the fruit over a plate and sprinkle
sugar over it. The plate will catch any
spilled sugar.

4 Place the fruit carefully on the doily.

5 Frost all the pieces of fruit in the same
way, arranging the larger pieces first, then
the smaller, to balance the composition.

6 Do not put the arrangement in the
refrigerator nor leave it in a place where
there is steam or the sugar will melt.

If you do not have a sugar sifter, use
a spoon to sprinkle on the sugar. Do
not dip fruits in sugar or it tends to
stick to the egg-white in lumps and
the soft, frosted look is lost.

## Frosted flowers
You can use frosted flowers for cake
and desserts decorations. Choose
fragrant flowers – miniature roses
and rose buds, rose petals, violets,
primroses, freesia, stephanotis,
orange blossom, florets of hyacinths
and crocus. Brush the flowers very
lightly with beaten egg-white then
dust with caster sugar and leave them
on greaseproof paper to dry for
about 1½ hours. Herbs leaves – mint,
borage, verbena etc – can also be
frosted and look pretty when
arranged with fruit desserts. Pick the
leaves and prepare them when they
are very fresh. Brush the leaves with
lightly beaten egg-white and dust
with sugar. Leave to dry. Frosted
leaves will not last for more than 24
hours.

# Christmas bandbox

*This arrangement with its bright colours, twirling ribbons and overflowing with tiny toys and gifts is an ideal centrepiece for a children's party.*

## Materials
A large, round cake or biscuit tin
Metallic paper (to cover the tin)
Satin and grosgrain ribbons, plains and
    stripes, in different widths
Latex adhesive
Florists foam
Gift tie ribbons in mixed colours
Florists stub wires
Christmas tree baubles
Coloured wooden beads
Coloured pipe-cleaners
Miniature toys, foil-wrapped candies
Florist's binding wire

## Preparation
**1** Cut the foam and fit it into the tin tightly.

## Working the design
**2** Cut a piece of metallic paper to the circumference of the tin plus ½in (1cm), by the depth plus ¾in (18mm). Stick the paper round the tin with the excess paper at the top.

**3** Snip into the excess paper all round and fold the tabs down. Stick them inside the tin.

**4** Cut strips of the plain and striped ribbons and stick one end to the inside top edge of the tin, the other end underneath.

**5** Curl pieces of gift tie ribbon ends over a scissors blade to curl them.

**6** Cut short lengths of wire. Twist wire round the ribbon curls to make two 'legs'. Push the wire ends into the foam. Allow some of the ribbon curls to fall over the edge of the bandbox.

**7** Thread beads onto pieces of pipe-cleaner and push them into the foam.

---

### Smart bandbox ideas
You can adapt the basic design for adult parties by using ribbons in more sophisticated colours. For a baby shower, use pale blue, pink, yellow and white ribbons and arrange small gifts in the bandbox – baby beads, diaper pins, tubes of cream, tiny soft toys, plastic bath toys and so on. Wedding anniversaries also lend themselves to this idea. For instance, red ribbons and baubles, together with small gifts in the same colour would make a superb centre piece for a ruby wedding party.

---

Stick strips of ribbon inside the top edge and to the bottom of the tin.

**8** Push the ends of stub wires through candy wrappers, twist the wire ends together so that there are two 'legs' and push the 'legs' into the foam.

**9** Having completed the colourful decorations, heap the toys and baubles on the bandbox and lift the ribbon curls, so that the foam is hidden.

# Mini-hamper

*What could be more exciting than a miniature hamper, full of ribbon-tied tiny boxes spilling out onto the party table? The boxes could contain little gifts for going-home presents for your guests.*

## Materials
Pattern paper
Thin card
Clear adhesive tape or quick-drying
  adhesive
Giftwrap papers with a small pattern
Narrow ribbons
Wicker basket with a hinged lid
Tissue paper

## Preparation
**1 Boxes** Trace the box pattern on paper. Transfer to thin card and cut out as many boxes as required. Score along the broken lines and fold the box sides and lid. Tape or stick the tabs to form the boxes. Insert small gifts at this stage if required.

### More ideas
Use the hamper centrepiece as a 'lucky dip' for your guests. Invite them to choose a parcel – both children and adults love a surprise. If a larger basket can be obtained, try painting it gold and then fill it with gold-wrapped gifts. Leave the lid slightly open. From each gift, trail a ribbon to each place setting and stick a tiny card with the guest's name to the end.

As an alternative to boxes, the hamper could be filled with special chocolates and candies.

**Trace the box pattern from this diagram. Score on the broken lines.**

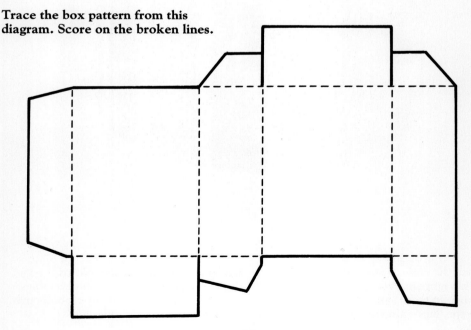

2 Wrap the boxes in giftwrap paper and tie with narrow ribbons.

**Working the design**
3 Shred the tissue paper. Put a layer of shreds in the bottom of the basket.

4 Top the tissue paper shreds with wrapped boxes. Some boxes could have tiny sprays of silk flowers added, tucked under the ribbons.

# Corn sheaf

*Tie a sheaf of corn, wheat or barley with crinkle ribbon, or a raffia plait, for a striking table decoration. A touch of colour might be added with small, artificial berries, wired onto long corn stalks.*

### Materials
A large bunch of corn, wheat or barley.
Crinkle ribbon, 2 yd (2.5m)
Skein of natural raffia (optional)
Fine string

### Preparation
1 If the seeds seem loose and tend to drop, spray the corn with hair lacquer or fixative.

### Working the design
2 Bind about three-quarters of the corn together to make the core of the sheaf.

3 Use the remaining corn to make the outer layer. Secure groups of stalks to the central core with string, binding high up under the heads.

4 Twist the outer layer to make a spiral effect.

5 Lay the sheaf on a flat surface and trim the ends level so that the sheaf will stand on its ends.

6 Open the crinkle ribbon and tie it round the sheaf, with a generous bow.

7 If you prefer a raffia plait, make a plait of 3 groups of 3 strands. Tie round the sheaf to cover the string.

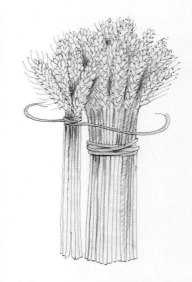

Secure the outer groups of corn stalks to the core with string.

### Sheaf of roses
Dried, stemmed roses also lend themselves to this style of arrangement. Most florists sell dried roses but they are simple to preserve at home. Choose flowers in bud and just opening. Crush a quantity of silica gel to powder (use a rolling pin wrapped in a cloth). Pour some of the powder into the bottom of a box long enough to take the roses with their stems. Arrange the roses on the surface then spoon powder between the petals and leaves. Cover the flowers completely. Cover the box and seal it. Leave the flowers to dry. When they feel papery and crisp (up to 7 days) remove the flowers.

# Ice bowl

*This unusual and stunning table centre takes time to make but it is well worth creating for a special anniversary. Use it for fresh fruit but not for liquids as these will melt the ice.*

**Materials**
A large glass bowl
A smaller glass bowl
Glass jar with beans or rice inside
Clear tape
Any of the following: small flower heads
  (small roses, nasturtiums,
  honeysuckle), leaves such as chicory,
  lamb's ear lettuce etc

**Preparation**
**1** Place the small bowl in the larger and pour water between the two until it comes to about ½in (1cm) from the rims.

**2** Stand the jar in the middle of the small bowl. The weight will help to keep the small bowl from moving around.

**3** Carefully tape the bowls and jar together.

**4** Place the bowls in the freezer for about 30 minutes or until ice begins to form.

An ice bowl makes a stunning centrepiece for a buffet table but take the precaution of standing it on a glass or silver serving dish or tray because, inevitably, the ice will slowly melt. Do not make the ice bowl more than two or three days in advance or the flowers and leaves may go brown. If you prefer, the flowers could be all of one colour – white looks superb – or you could try the effect of seasonal fruits with their leaves, such as strawberries.

**Working the design**
**5** Remove the bowls from the freezer. Remove the holding tapes. Insert flowers and leaves into the partly frozen water between the bowls, pushing it down with a knitting needle.

Tape the bowls and jar together so that they do not move around.

Push flowers and leaves into the water between the two bowls.

**6** Re-tape the bowls together. Return the bowls to the freezer and freeze overnight.

**7** Remove the tape and the jar. Lower the large bowl into a bigger container of cold water (the water must not spill over the edge). Pour water into the smaller bowl. In a little while, the small bowl will lift away from the ice lining and the bigger bowl can be eased off, leaving an ice bowl.

**8** Place the bowl on a plate and fill with flowers or fresh fruits.

**Sugar baskets**

These make effective containers for displaying sweets or frosted fruits. Make a syrup by boiling 4 tbls of caster sugar with 2 tbls of water. Dip a large crocheted mat into the syrup. Squeeze out the excess. Arrange the mat over an upturned bowl. Smooth down the sides and spread the decorative edges. Leave to dry in a warm place. Ease the basket from the mould. Spray with varnish, brush silver or gold paint on the basket.

# Golden fruit

*This sensational centrepiece is made from plastic fruit and leaves which have been sprayed gold.It could make the focal point of an all-gold party table. Real, gold-sprayed nuts could be added.*

## Materials
Gold doily; cake stand or plate
Plastic fruit and leaves
Gold spray paint
Quick-drying adhesive

## Preparation
**1** Place the doily on the cake stand or plate.

## Working the design
**2** Spray the leaves and fruit gold, working in the open air if possible and over a large sheet of newspaper.

**3** Leave sprayed pieces to dry then turn them over and spray any unpainted places.

**4** Arrange leaves round the cake stand or plate, fixing them in place with a touch of adhesive.

**5** Arrange the larger pieces of fruit in the middle of the leaves. Stick them down if necessary. Then add the smaller pieces, heaping them until you have a pleasing arrangement. Try to ensure that the best side of the fruit shows and that any seams in the plastic are hidden with more leaves.

## Spray painting
This can be dangerous if done inside the house and is a messy business even when you are working outside. Make yourself a spraying booth from an empty cardboard box. Place the item to be painted inside and spray. The box will contain the area of the spray.

# Party poppies

*Bright paper poppies make a cheerful display for a teenage party. For unusual containers, stand the poppies in empty blue or green mineral water bottles.*

**Materials**
Tracing paper
Double-sided crepe paper (red, yellow or
    orange)
Black watercolour paint or crayon
Florists' stub wires, 12–15in (30–37.5cm)
    long
Cotton wool
Florists' binding wire
Black crêpe paper
Florists' green stem tape

**Preparation**
1 Trace the poppy petal pattern on folded paper. Cut out and use the pattern to cut 6 petals from crêpe paper with the direction arrow lying along the grain.

**Working the design**
2 Curve and cup each petal by holding it between thumbs and forefingers and stretching from the centre outwards. Using black paint, brush strokes from the bottom end of each petal.

3 Cut a 1 × 8in (2.5 × 20cm) strip of black paper on the cross grain. Cut a ½in (1cm) fringe on the grain along one edge.

4 **Assembling the poppy** Bend a hook on one end of a stub wire. Thread binding wire through the hook and twist it round the stem. Leave a wire end.

5 Cover the hook with cotton wool. Bind it securely with the wire.

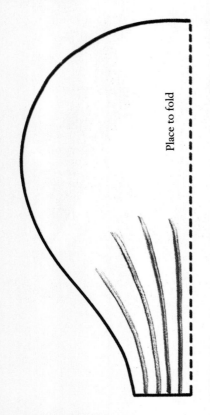

Place to fold

**Trace this petal on folded pattern paper.**

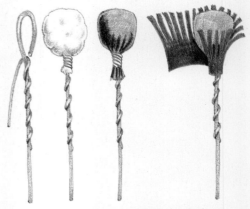

Bend a hook on the stub wire and thread binding wire through. Cover the hook with cotton wool. Wire the black fringe round.

**6** Cut a circle of black crêpe paper, wrap it over the wool and wire round the stem securely.

**7** Gather the black paper fringe in the fingers and wire this round the outside of the black poppy centre.

**8** Take each petal in turn, pleat the bottom end and wire round the poppy centre, overlapping each petal slightly.

**9** Cover the stem with stem tape, twisting the stem in your fingers as you work. Arrange the poppies in a container.

**10** If you like, cut leaves from two-tone green crêpe paper and tape to the stem as you cover it.

# Room Decorations

# Pine-cone tree

*Here is a novel way of using pine-cones collected on autumn walks. A tree-shaped base is used here but the method could be adapted to bases of other shapes.*

## Materials
Pattern paper
Plywood or hardboard, 20 × 18in (50 × 45cm)
Approximately 80 small pine-cones
Quick-drying glue
Clear varnish
Wire hanging
Tartan ribbon
Cinnamon sticks, broken into short lengths
Narrow red ribbon
Small foil-wrapped gifts (or boxes)
Small gold baubles; artificial red berries

## Preparation
**1** Spread the cones on a baking tray and put them in a hot oven for 20 minutes. This will remove any moisture from them – and kill any hidden insects.

Wire cinnamon stick bundles, baubles and boxes.

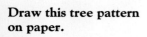
**Draw this tree pattern on paper.**

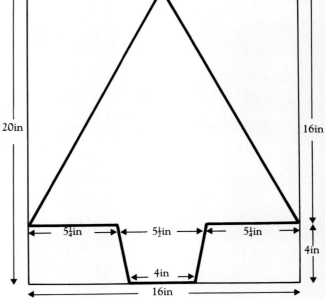

20in

16in

5¼in    5½in    5¼in

4in

4in

16in

2 Draw the tree shape from the diagram pattern and transfer onto the plywood or hardboard. Cut out the shape.

3 Drill 2 holes at the top for the hanger.

**Working the design**
4 Thread wire through the holes from the back and twist them together at the front for a hanger.

5 Starting at the top of the tree, stick the pine-cones to the tree shape to cover the surface. Leave to dry.

6 When the glue is dry, paint all over the cones with varnish.

7 Tie tartan ribbon bows and glue these between the pine-cones.

8 Tie bundles of 3 cinnamon sticks and twist a wire through the ribbon. Push between the cones.

9 Wire the gift boxes, baubles and berries in the same way and push between the cones.

# Anniversary heart

*Celebrate a silver wedding anniversary with a fragrant heart decoration, trimmed with silver ribbons. The heart pictured is 12 × 10in (30 × 25cm) but the heart can be made to any size.*

## Materials
Bunches of dried lavender (about 10)
Florists' green stem tape
Florists' stub wires, 12in (30cm) long, 22 gauge
Silver stub wires, 28 gauge
Reel of florists' binding wire
Silver grosgrain ribbon, ⅜in (9mm) wide
Wide satin ribbon

## Preparation
1 To make the basic wire shape, hold four stiff stub wires together with the ends at different levels. Tape them together, working up the wires. As you come to the end of the first wire, introduce another and continue binding. Introduce new wires as you go, always keeping the total to four. Work until the basic wire is about 1¼yd (1m) long.

2 Trim the last wire ends and tape neatly. Bend the ends towards each other to form a heart shape. Tape the ends together.

## Working the design
3 Trim the lavender stalks to within 2in (5cm) of the heads. Bind groups of 6 stems together with wire.

4 Starting in the middle of the indentation at the top of the heart shape, bind bunches of lavender to the base wire, so that the heads lie in opposite directions on each side. Wire one bunch on top of the base wire and one underneath.

5 Work down both sides of the heart to the bottom.

6 Tie ribbon bows round the wreath at intervals. Tie a large ribbon bow to the bottom of the heart.

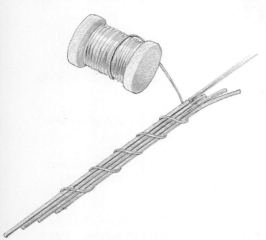

Bind the 4 wires with stem tape introducing additional wires as required.

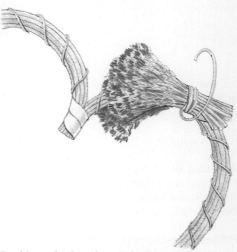

Bind lavender bunches to the heart shape, starting at the top.

# Muslin-swagged table

*Decorating large areas of table for an event such as a Christening, wedding or an anniversary party can be rather costly in the amount of fabric required. Here is a pretty styling idea using muslin.*

**Materials**
White sheeting
Muslin
White or cream dress net
Fresh or silk flowers; greenery
Florists' binding wire
Narrow, white or cream satin ribbons

**Preparation**
1  Cover the table with white sheeting. Over this, spread the muslin so that it overhangs by about 12in (30cm).

To develop the decorative idea, cut a large square of muslin. Cut a small hole in the middle. Hang the square over a shallow, white lampshade to hang over the table. Arrange trailing flowers, ribbons and ivy over the shade. For safety, use only very low wattage electric bulbs in fabric-draped lights.

Gather up the overhang and pin into swags round the table.

**2** Gather up the overhang to form evenly spaced swags, and pin them to the white sheeting to hold them in place.

**Working the design**
**3** Using a second piece of muslin, pin one end to the tablecloth at the back of the table. Make swags round the table to lie over the earlier swags. Pin the new swags to the tablecloth edge as before.

**4** Twist strips of net round the swags.

**5** Wire sprays of flowers and greenery. Tie them to the swags at the edge of the table with ribbons.

# Salt dough decorations

*Salt dough is very easy to model and, once baked and varnished, the decorations will last for many years. Salt dough pieces are painted and varnished after baking.*

**Materials**
3 cups of plain flour
1 cup of salt
1 teaspoon of glycerine
1 cup of warm water
Paper clip
Paints, clear varnish
Narrow ribbons

**Preparation**
1 Dissolve the salt in the warm water (this helps to make the dough smoother in texture). Leave the water to cool.

2 Sieve the flour into the bowl, add the glycerine.

3 Pour in the salt water, stirring all the time, to make a soft dough.

4 Remove the dough from the bowl and knead, as though you were making bread.

**GARLAND**
5 Place a plate face downwards on a baking tray, with enough room round the plate to build up the garland. (The plate can be removed afterwards.)

6 Break off a 2 pieces of dough and roll 2 long, fat, sausage shapes.

7 Twist the ropes together round a plate, placed on a baking tray. Dampen the ends to join them.

8 Model a variety of small fruits. Roll holly berry balls and pierce them with a knitting needle.

9 Using a sharp knife, cut several holly leaves from rolled-out dough.

10 Stick the fruits, berries and leaves to the garland with a little water.

11 Push a paper clip halfway into the back of the garland for a hanger. Remove the plate if you like.

12 **Baking** Leave the garland to stand, overnight if possible. Set the oven at a very low temperature – 250°F (130°C), gas mark ½. Bake for 30 minutes, then turn the oven up to 300°F (150°C), gas mark 2.

13 The salt dough must be baked very slowly, without colouring and the time it takes depends on the thickness of the piece. The garland may take between 3 and 4 hours. Lift the piece from the baking tray and tap the back. It should be quite hard.

Twist the dough ropes round the plate. Dampen the ends to join them.

**14 Decorating** The garland must be quite cold before starting the decoration. Paint the fruits, leaves and berries with water colour paints, poster paints or acrylic colours. When the paint is dry, brush with clear varnish front and back. Give the garland a second coat when the first is dry.

**TREE DECORATIONS**
1 Prepare and roll out the salt dough.

2 Using fancy pastry cutters (stars, Christmas tree, bells etc) cut out the shapes and lift them carefully onto a baking tray. Pierce holes near the top with a skewer.

3 Bake the decorations in a cool oven for about 30 minutes.

4 When cool, decorate the pieces with poster paints, varnish on both sides and leave to dry.

5 Thread narrow, ⅛in (3mm)-wide ribbons through the holes for hanging. Knot the ribbon ends.

# Fold and cut decorations

*With just coloured paper and scissors, you can make a variety of chain decorations to suit every occasion. Here are Hallowe'en designs for a pumpkin, witch's cat, skull and cross bones and a bat.*

## Materials
Tracing paper
Card for templates
Cartridge or crêpe paper
Quick-drying adhesive (optional)

## Preparation
**1** The secret of good chain-making is crisply folded paper. The length of the paper you use depends on how long the chain needs to span. Strips can be joined by sticking the ends together. Cut a strip of paper deep enough to take your chosen design plus 1in (2.5cm).

**2** Trace the designs and then transfer them to cardboard. Cut out for a template.

## Working the design
**3** First, fold the paper strip. Make the first fold to the width of the chosen design. The broken lines (see patterns) will align with the folded edges. Turn the strip over and make another fold. Continue, folding and turning, making concertina-folds along the strip. Make sure you crease each fold firmly.

When planning party decorations choose paper colours suitable for the occasion – black, red and orange for Hallowe'en, red and green for Christmas, yellow, white and green for Easter. The shapes can be decorated with stick-on stars or spots, or with felt-tip designs.

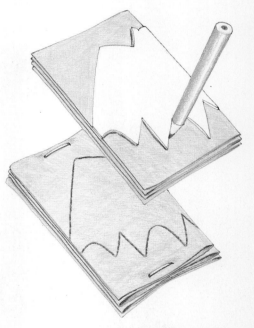

Place the template on the folded strip and trace around. Staple the layers together.

**4** Place the template on the folded strip so that there is ½in (1cm) above and below the template. Pencil round the design. Staple the paper layers together, top and bottom.

**5** Cut out, through all layers, on the solid lines. Make sure that you do not cut the broken lines. Remove the staples.

**6** Open the strip. Tape the chain to walls, mirrors, windows or doors – or stick several strips together and hang the the chain across the room.

# Floating candles

*There is something quite magical about the effect of candles floating in water and they make a wonderful centrepiece. They can last for two or three hours.*

## Materials
(To make 8 floating candles)
2lb 3oz (1kg) of wax granules
Wicks, $\frac{1}{2}$in (1cm) size
$\frac{1}{4}$ disc of pink or red wax pigment

## Preparation
1  Melt the wax gently in a double boiler to 160°F (71°C). Use a thermometer to check the temperature. Add the dye disc fragment to the melted wax and stir to distribute the colour evenly.

2  Cut 8 pieces of wick, 2in (5cm) long. Dip the wicks in the wax and lay aside.

## Working the design
3  When the wax is the correct temperature, pour out some of the wax onto greaseproof paper (use a ladle) so that it forms a pool about $\frac{1}{4}$in (6mm) thick.

4  Leave the wax until it is partially set and rubbery. Using a pastry cutter, cut out circles about 2in (5cm) diameter. Pierce a hole in the middle of each and insert a wick. Drip a little wax round the wick to fill the hole.

5  Check the remaining wax to see that it is not overheating. Try and keep it at the correct temperature. Pour out more wax onto greaseproof paper. When it is rubbery, cut 2 or 3 small petal shapes, using a scalpel knife. and squeeze them round the wick.

Pour melted wax onto greaseproof paper. When almost cool, cut out circles.

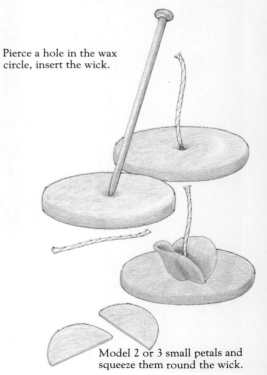

Pierce a hole in the wax circle, insert the wick.

Model 2 or 3 small petals and squeeze them round the wick.

**6** Cut larger petals and curve them in your fingers. Set them round the wick fixing in place with melted wax. Work as quickly as you can. If the wax cools too much, you can soften it with a hairdryer.

**7** Build up the flower shape round the wick – you will probably need 8–10 petals of different sizes. Leave the candles to cool. Trim the wicks to $\frac{1}{2}$in (1cm) before lighting them. Float the candles in water.

THREE

# Table Settings

# Tussie mussie

*These simple nosegays of dried flowers and herbs are fragrant and look very pretty on a dinner table setting. They make a pleasant gift for your guests to take away after the party.*

## Materials
For one tussie mussie:
Large paper doily
White dressmaking net
Florists' wire
Florists' stem tape (green or white)
Dried flowers and herbs, leaves with
    stems, or fresh flowers and foliage
Double-faced satin ribbon, ½in (1cm) wide
Stick adhesive (optional)

## Preparation
1 Trim the decorative edge from the doily. Cut a 6in (15cm) circle of white net. Stick the doily edge round the circle. Fold the net into four and snip off the point. Cut a strip of net about 4in (10cm) deep by 6in (15cm).

## Working the design
2 Take 3 or 4 stems of foliage and slip them through the hole in the net circle. Push the circle up under the leaves. Insert flowers, so that they are surrounded by leaves. (If you have one flower that is larger than the others, such as a rose, put this in the middle.)

3 Insert more flowers and pieces of foliage so that you have an arrangement that is higher in the centre than at the sides. Trim the stems so that they are all the same length.

4 Bind the stems together with wire, starting high up, under the net frill and close to the flower heads.

5 If you are using fresh flowers, cover the stems with florists' tape to help to retain their moisture.

6 Wrap the net strip the bound stems. Use a touch of adhesive to hold it in place if necessary.

7 Tie satin ribbon round the tussie mussie.

Stick the doily edging round the net circle.

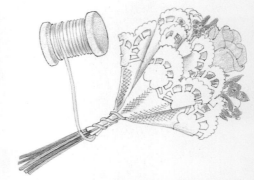

Bind the stems together with wire, starting high up under the net circle.

# Children's Easter party

*Children of all ages love the spring celebration and little baskets of chocolate eggs topped with chicks and rabbits will add to their excitement. Arrange a basket at each place.*

## Materials
Place mats
Pattern paper
Card for a template
Yellow and white felt, 12in (30cm)
  squares
Stick adhesive
Satin ribbons, ricrac braid
### Chicks and rabbits
Small baskets
Yellow and white tissue paper
Yellow, white and blue double knitting
  yarn
Stiff card
Yellow and white pipe-cleaners
Scraps of black wool (or small black
  beads)
Scraps of pale blue, pink and yellow felt
Fabric adhesive
Ribbons for trimming

## PLACE MATS
### Preparation
**1** Draw a 9 × 6in (22.5 × 15cm) rectangle on pattern paper. Round off the ends to make an egg shape. Transfer to card and cut out for a template.

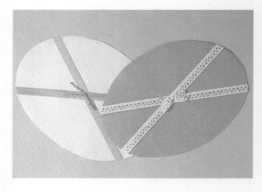

**2** Place the template on the felt and cut out as many shapes as required.

### Working the design
**3** Decorate the table mats with strips of ribbon and ricrac braid, to look like Easter eggs. Stick the ribbon in place.

## POMPON CHICKS AND RABBITS
### Preparation
**1** Draw a 6in (15cm)-diameter circle on paper and, using it as a pattern, cut out 2 card circles. Cut a 1in (2.5cm)-diameter hole in the middle of both.

### Working the design
**2** Knot the 2 card rings together with the wool end. Unroll a long length and wind a ball that will slip through the hole easily. Wind wool over the rings, working round so that the strands lie evenly, until the hole is filled. Wind as many small balls of yarn as you require. Thread the wool into a bodkin for the last windings, and push this through the hole. The more wool you can get onto the rings, the better the finished pompon.

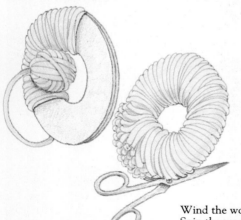

Wind the wool round the card rings.
Snip the wool strands from the card rings.

**3** With pointed scissors, snip the strands on the edges of the rings. The wool will spring away from the card and you will be able to tie wool between the card rings and round the 'waist' of the ball.

**4** Gently tear the card rings away from the ball. Trim the ball if necessary.

**5 Chick** Make a large yellow pompon and a smaller pompon on a 4in (10cm)-diameter card ring. Stick it to the larger ball for a head. Cut a diamond shape from yellow felt for a beak. Sew or stick the beak into the head. Work eyes from French knots, using black wool – or sew small beads into the head.

**6** Make legs by bending a yellow pipe-cleaner in half. Sew it to the underside of the body. Bend the ends to make feet.

**7 Rabbits** These are made in the same way as the chicks. Make a large white pompon for the body and a smaller white pompon for the head. Make a tiny blue pompon for a tail on $\frac{3}{4}$in (18mm) card circles. Cut 2 blue felt ears for each rabbit and stick in place on the head. Stick the tail to the body. Make the eyes as you did for the chicks. Cut a tiny pink circle for the nose and stick to the face. Bend a white pipe-cleaner in half then bend the ends in for about 1in (2.5cm) to make paws. Sew the paws under the front body.

**Finishing**
**8** Shred tissue paper and put a little into each basket. Put chocolate eggs on the tissue, top with a chick or rabbit. Trim the baskets with ribbon or a few artificial flowers if desired.

47

# Folded napkins

*Decoratively folded napkins are a simple way of making a table look festive. For the best effect, napkins should be made of good quality damask and well-starched.*

## CANDLE

**1** Fold the napkin diagonally into a triangle.

**2** Fold up the folded edge.

**3** Turn the napkin over and roll it firmly from the left-hand corner.

**4** Tuck the right-hand corner into the folded edge to keep the roll tight. The napkin should stand on end. Fold one of the points down. The other simulates the flame.

**Changing times**
In 1881, in her book of household management, Mrs Beeton gave her readers more than a dozen different ways of folding 'serviettes' but commented that 'fancy designs are not fashionable in the household now and serviettes should be simply be folded neatly and placed on the plate'.

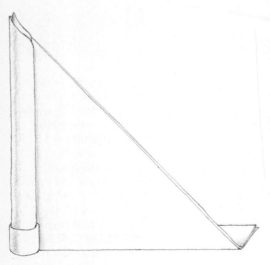

Roll the napkin firmly.

Tuck the corner into the fold.

Turn a point down.

When you are folding napkins into a style, spray the napkin with starch and hot-iron the creases into the fabric as you work.

## LOTUS BLOSSOM

**1** Fold the four corners of the napkin to the centre. Turn the napkin over.

**2** Fold the corners of the new square to the centre.

**3** Turn the napkin over again and fold the corners to the centre again.

**4** Holding the centre with the fingers (or a small wine glass) reach under the napkin and gently pull out the corners so that they peak and stand away. This design is particularly good for containing a bread roll.

## FAN

**1** Working from the diagram, fold napkin side C – D up towards A – B, but about 1¼in (3cm) below A – B.

**2** Now fold C – D down so that it is about 1in (2.5cm) above the fold.

**3** Fold A – B down so that the edge lies above C – D.

**4** Pleat the napkin lengthways. Turn the front layer edge forward a little.

**5** Slip a pencil through the middle, folded pleats to puff them up a little.

## THE WAVE

**1** Fold the napkin into three to make a rectangle.

**2** Fold in the short sides so that the folds lie at the middle. Turn the napkin over.

50

**Lotus blossom**

Fold the napkin, fold in the short sides, fold from the right.

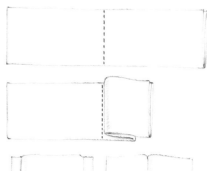

**3** Fold the right-hand side over so that the 'waves' rise.

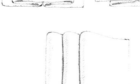

## Lotus blossom

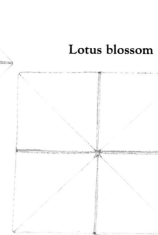

Fold the corners to the centre.

Turn the napkin over, fold in the corners again.

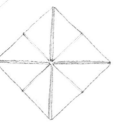

Fold the new corners to the centre.

## FLEUR-DE-LYS

**1** Fold the napkin in half diagonally.

**2** With the folded edge lying away from you, bring the bottom corner up so that it overlaps the folded edge.

**3** Turn the napkin over and fold up the other corner.

**4** Concertina-pleat the napkin from left to right.

**5** Place the napkin in a wine glass. Pull the front point forwards.

**Fleur-de-lys**

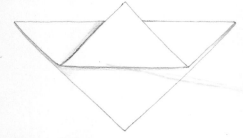

Bring up the bottom corner.

Fold up the other corner.

Concertina-pleat the napkin.

**Fleur-de-lys**

For some kinds of parties, paper napkins or serviettes are quite acceptable and, where children are involved, practical! The simpler folding designs will work with paper napkins, if they are of the quality where there are two or more layers of paper. Use an iron to get good, sharp creases. White napkins look fresh and clean but you may want to choose pastels or a strong, fashionable colour, to suit your party theme.

## THE POCKET

**1** Fold the napkin in half then in half again to form a square.

**2** Fold diagonally to make a triangle.

**3** With the fold lying towards you, fold down the top layer several times so that it forms a cuff across the fold.

**4** Without creasing, fold each of the remaining corners down in turn.

**5** Slip a posy of fresh or dried flowers – or a small gift, such as a lacy handkerchief – into the pocket.

Fold the top layer down to form a cuff.

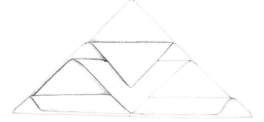

Fold each corner down in turn.

**The pocket**

53

## Festive tables

For an original and personalized party table, stencil motifs on the tablecloth and napkins. There are a of ready-made stencils in holiday themes in the shops or you can cut your own from stencil blanks. Motifs can be found on giftwrap and greetings cards and there are also some good designs in this book. Retrace the motif on to the stencil blank using typists' carbon paper and cut out with a sharp crafts knife.

Fabric paints are ideal for stencilling and come in a wide range of colours. Stretch the fabric on a surface protected with newspaper. Hold the edges down with masking tape. Use a stubby stencilling brush and mix the paint on the dry side. Tape the stencil in position and dab paint through the holes. Lift the stencil off carefully. Leave each colour to dry before applying the next.

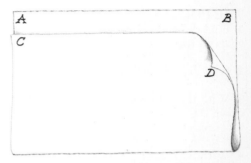

Fold C – D up to A – B and just below the edge.

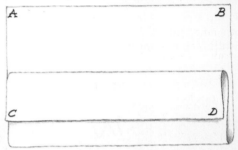

Fold down C – D.

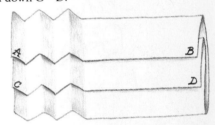

Fold down A – B, pleat the napkin lengthways.

## Fan

### Napkin rings

Fancy napkin rings are an easy way of dressing up table napkins and you can vary the trimmming to suit the occasion.

**Sea theme** Roll the napkin into three, thread some shells onto shirring elastic and tie the elastic round the napkin. The napkin can be laid on scallop shells and decorated with a gypsophila spray.

**Ribbon and roses** Roll the napkin. Tie a piece of wide satin ribbon round the middle in a double knot. Cut the ribbon ends diagonally. Thread a short length of ribbon under the knot and tie once, again cutting the ends diagonally. Slip a fresh rose under the knot.

**Country style** Form a cardboard ring and tape the join. Cover the ring with checked fabric or felt. Trim the edges with braid.

**Bridal ring** Twist 2 florists' stub wires into a ring. Cover with white florists' stem tape. Wire small silk flowers round the ring. Wind white ribbon round the ring between the flowers, covering the wires. Tie bows of narrow cream ribbon round the ring between the flowers.

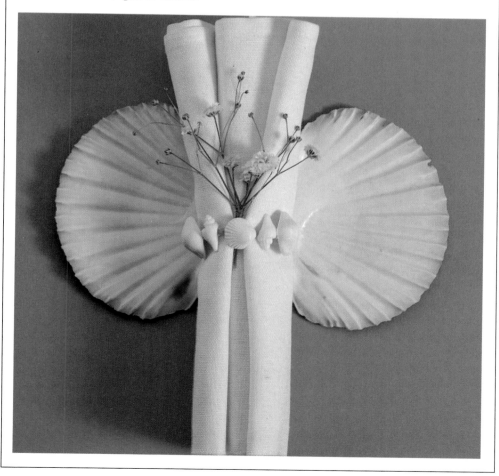

# New Year celebration

*Colourful and chic, tartan patterns are just the thing for*
*New Year decorations. Here are some ideas for table decor using*
*tartan-patterned ribbons, fabric and paper.*

## Materials
### Place cards
Red and green shiny surfaced card
Stick adhesive
Taffeta ribbon, ¼in (6mm) wide
Red or gold cord
Gold marker pen
### Place mats
Tartan-patterned paper
### Napkins
(For 6 place settings)
Tartan-patterned cotton fabric
Ribbons as follows (for 6 place settings):
   18in (45cm) of 2in (10cm)-wide red/
   green striped grosgrain ribbon (napkin
   loops); 3yd (2.80cm) of 1½in (3.5cm)-
   wide taffeta tartan ribbon (napkin
   bows)
Kilt pins, sprigs of heather

## Preparation
### PLACE CARDS
1 For each place card, cut a rectangle of
card 4in (10cm) wide by 5in (12.5cm)
deep. Working on the shiny, coloured
side, score across the middle of the card,
using a crafts knife tip, very lightly. Aim
to just break the coloured surface.

---

> **Neat place mats**
> Paper place mats will last longer if
> you first laminate the paper to
> strong, flexible card by spraying the
> surface with varnish and applying the
> paper. Then cut out the mats. For a
> pretty effect, stick a piece of red or
> gold gift tie cord round the edges,
> finishing the ends in a bow.

---

## Working the design
2 Cut 2 4in(10cm) strips of narrow,
tartan ribbon and 2 2½in (6cm) strips.
Spread stick adhesive on the back of the
ribbon strips and stick them round the
edges of the front of the card,
overlapping at the corners. (If you prefer,
you could cut strips of the tartan-
patterned paper and use these instead).

Stick ribbon strips round the front of the place
card, overlapping at the corners.

Stitch the ends of the striped ribbon, flatten the
ring. Use on both ladies and men's table napkins.

**3** Leave to dry before folding the card. Tie a small red or gold cord bow. Stick to one corner. Write the guest's name in gold pen. If you like, you could replace the bow with a small sprig of white heather.

## PLACE MATS
**4** Cut 16in (40cm)-diameter circles of paper for each place mat.

## TABLE NAPKINS
**5** For each napkin, cut rectangles 15 × 12in (42.5 × 30cm). Turn a narrow hem on all four sides of the fabric squares, press and then zigzag-stitch neatly.

**Finishing and assembling**
**6** Fold ladies' napkins in half, then roll loosely. Tie with a tartan ribbon, the bow on the top. Zizag-stitch the ends of the striped ribbon together, overlapping them. Flatten the ribbon ring, then slip the ribbon under the tartan bow to lie on the napkin. Tuck a sprig of white heather under the bow.

**7** For the men's napkins, fold them in half then roll loosely. Tie round with tartan ribbon. Make another loop of the striped ribbon and slip under the bow. Tie another bow of tartan ribbon round both the first bow. Fix a kilt pin across the bows.

# Sugared almond gift parcels

*In many European countries, a gift of sugared almonds is given to guests at the Christening or naming of a baby. Pretty, ribbon-trimmed parcels of the sweets makes a charming presentation.*

## Materials
Stiff dress net, pink, white or blue, 10in (25cm) squares, 2 for each parcel
Clear nail polish
Silver glitter dust
Sugared almonds
Satin ribbons or gift tie ribbons
Pearl sequins (optional)
Silk flowers (optional)

## Preparation
1 Use a plate to cut a 10in (25cm)-diameter circle from paper. Pin 4 squares of net together, in the middle and round the edges. Pin the pattern to the net and cut out. Cut 2 net circles for each parcel, either white and pink, white and blue, pink and blue or 2 circles of the same colour.

## Working the design
2 Pour a little glitter dust onto a piece of paper on a plate. Fold each net circle in half, then quarters, then eighths, then fold once again. Brush nail polish on the cut edges – take care not to apply too much or let drips fall.

3 Dip the sticky edges of the net into the glitter dust. Shake off the excess. Stand the still-folded circle in a cup while it dries. Decorate all the circles in the same way.

4 Spread two circles of net one on the other. Place 6–8 almonds in the middle. Draw up the sides and tie tightly with narrow ribbon, finishing with a bow.

5 If you are using silk flowers, slip the stems under the ribbon.

6 If you like, pearlized sequins can be stuck to the outside of the parcels.

Dip the folded circle into the glitter dust.

---

### More ideas
Instead of sequins, stick tiny guipure lace daisies to the net.
For a special gift, tie a silver good luck charm to each parcel.
Use this idea for a wedding buffet also. Have small, silver-edged cards printed with the bride and groom's names and the date. Tie a card to each parcel.

# National holiday party

*For sheer impact, there is nothing like bright, primary colours for a party scheme. Here are some ideas for a holiday celebration party – you could substitute any national flag colours.*

**Materials**
**Tablecloth**
Tracing paper
Stencil blank (or thin card)
White cotton fabric
Fabric paint, stencilling brush
**Table napkins**
Coloured cotton fabric, 12in (30cm)
   squares
**You will also need:**
White and coloured candles
White and coloured satin, or gift,
   ribbons
Streamers etc (optional)

**Trace this half-star
on folded paper.**

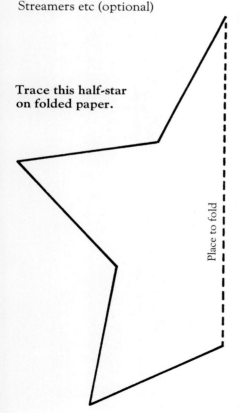

Place to fold

**TABLE-CLOTH**
**Preparation**
1 Iron the creases from the fabric. Trace the star pattern. Transfer to the stencil blank and cut out.

2 Mix the fabric paint according to the manufacturer's instructions. It should be fairly dry for stencilling.

**Working the design**
3 Spread the fabric on several sheets of newspaper. Tape it to the work surface at the edges. Position the stencil for the first motif.

4 Hold the stencil firmly in place. (If you prefer, you can tape it down.) Dip the stencil brush in the paint and then dab it once or twice on scrap paper to distribute the colour through the bristles. Dab the colour onto the fabric, starting in the middle of the motif and working outwards towards the edges of the stencil. Use only enough paint to colour the fabric – do not be tempted to use a lot of paint or it will soak the fabric and seep under the stencil.

5 Leave the stencil in place for a minute or two then carefully lift it from the fabric. Clean off the paint with a damp rag. Position the stencil for the next motif. Stencil the next star in the same way. Work stars all over the cloth and leave it until the paint is completely dry.

6 Fix the fabric paint according to the manufacturer's instructions.

7 Finish the cloth edges with a narrow, machine-stitched hem.

## CANDLE MATS

**8** Use the star pattern to cut shapes from glossy-surfaced card. (Alternatively, paint white card.) When cutting the star shapes, use a sharp, pointed scalpel knife and make the cuts against a metal-edged ruler. Cut gently for the first cut, drawing the knife towards the star point, then press harder for the second cut, cutting through the card. Cut each star arm from the centre towards the point.

## NAPKINS

**9** Turn and zigzag-stitch a narrow hem on all four sides. If you prefer a larger napkin, cut 16in (40cm) squares.

### Finishing and assembly

**10** Spread the stencilled cloth on the table. Arrange the candle mats, fix the candles to the mats with a little melted wax. Fold the table napkins and tie with ribbons or gift ties, finishing with a bow. Arrange ribbons or streamers across the table, between plates and glasses.

Tape, or hold, the stencil on the fabric firmly and dab on the paint.

# Sweet hearts

*What could be simpler – or prettier – that heart-shaped baskets filled with tiny sweets. They would make an ideal table decoration for any romantic occasion such as St Valentine's day celebrations.*

**Materials**
Heart-shaped baskets
Paper doilies
Tissue paper
Small sweets, chocolates or candies
Ribbons, artificial flowers etc

**Preparation**
1 If you like, sponge a little water-colour over the outside of the baskets, or paint them gold.

2 Shred the tissue paper.

**Working the design**
3 Arrange the doily in the basket so that the frilly edge shows.

4 Fill the bottom of the basket with shredded tissue.

5 Arrange sweets, chocolates or candies on the shredded tissue. Decorate the basket by twisting ribbon round the handle, or by fixing a bow to the top, or side, of the heart. Tuck tiny sprays of silk flowers into the basket edges if you like.

**Shredding paper**
You will need a very sharp pair of scissors for this – and a lot of patience. Cut a sheet of tissue paper in half, then half again, and again until you have squares about 6 × 6in (15 × 15cm). Take about 6 squares and roll them up loosely. Hold the roll with an elastic band. Flatten the roll and begin cutting 'slices' from the roll end, not more than ⅛in (3mm) wide. Work slowly and carefully. If you like, have three different colours of tissue, 2 of each in the roll.

**Plaited baskets**
Small, round baskets can be created from white plastic bags – inexpensive and a good re-cycling project. Cut the plastic into 1in (2.5cm)-wide strips and plait three together. Secure the ends with silver thread. Wind one end of the plait into a circle and sew the edges together with silver thread to form a disc. Continue, winding the plait round, sewing the edges together to make the basket sides. Tuck the finishing end to the inside and catch down. Sew on sequins etc to decorate.
  Plaited plastic can also be used to make decorations for a Christmas tree – an ideal project for children.

Roll the tissue loosely and cut into shreds.

# Pretty place cards

*Decorative place cards can set the mood of your party. Amusing, colourful shapes and figures delight children while festive-looking motifs create a Christmas party theme.*

**Materials**
Good-quality, smooth-surfaced coloured cartridge paper
Sticky-backed coloured paper
Sticky-back stars
Felt-tipped pens
You will also need a metal edged ruler, sharp crafts knife, scoring tool and sharp scissors

**Preparation**
1 Measure and mark the dimension of the place cards on the sheet of card. Measure accurately and make sure corners are exactly square. An ideal size for a place card, folded, is 4 × 3in (10 × 7.5cm), so measure rectangles 8 × 3in (20 × 7.5cm). However, place cards can be any shape or size you desire.

2 Measure and mark the middle of the paper across the width. Holding the ruler along the marks, draw the scoring tool across. This breaks the surface tension of the paper and the place card will fold cleanly.

**Working the designs**
3 **Hallowe'en party** Make the card from black paper. Score and fold. Trace the pumpkin motif and transfer onto orange paper. Cut out. Stick the pumpkin to the front of the folded card.

4 **Easter party** Make the card from green paper. Score and fold. Trace the egg shape and transfer to yellow paper. Cut out the egg. Trace and cut out the ribbon bow from white paper. Stick the bow on the egg and colour it with felt-tipped pens. Stick the egg to the front of the card.

**5 Christmas party** Make the card from dark blue paper. Score and fold. Trace the candle and cut the candle itself from red paper. Cut out the larger, yellow flame and the smaller, orange flame. Stick the orange flame on the yellow flame, then stick the flame behind the candle. Stick the candle to the card. Decorate with stick-on stars.

**Quick menu cards**
Save seasonal or occasional greeting cards and trim the picture to fit into a two-fold window card blank. Handwrite the menu inside the card in gold pen. Add the date of the occasion at the bottom corner.

Trace these patterns for place cards.

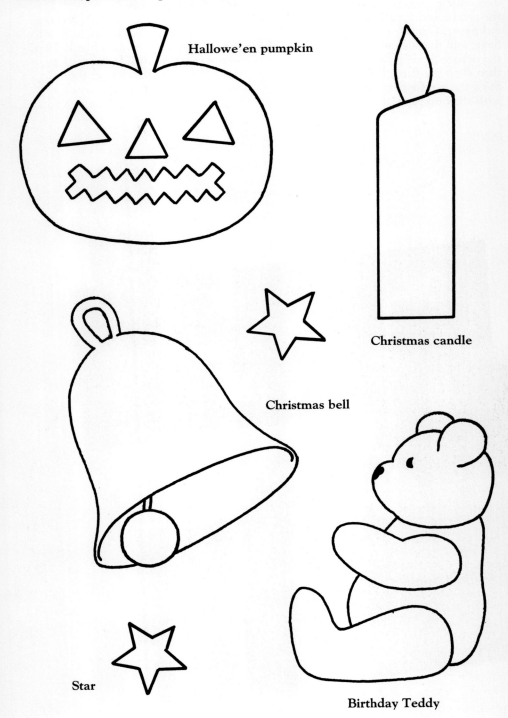

Hallowe'en pumpkin

Christmas candle

Christmas bell

Star

Birthday Teddy

**Wedding or Christening swan**

 **Stars**

**Sticky-backed paper**
This easy-to-use crafts paper is
usually sold in mixed-colour packets
of 8in (20cm) square sheets. To
reproduce a design, first trace each
area of colour separately. Transfer
the shapes onto the right side of the
coloured paper, using typist's carbon
paper. Cut out the shapes with a
small pair of scissors. Arrange the
pieces on the work surface, so that
you can see which pieces should
overlap. Dampen the back of the
shapes with a moistened piece of
cotton wool (use a cotton bud for
very tiny pieces). Position the shapes
on the chosen background.

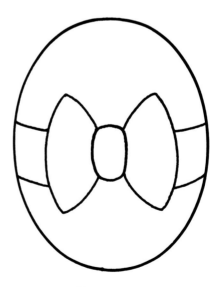

**Easter egg**

# Little boxes

*Small decorated boxes have dozens of uses in party decorations. Apart from being used to contain sweets for the table, they are also perfect containers for Christmas tree gifts.*

**Materials**

Matchbox trays (or make your own
  boxes)
Good quality, stiff card for boxes
Quick-drying adhesive
Patterned giftwrap
Spray adhesive
Lacy paper doilies
Stiff gift ribbon
Decorations such as narrow satin ribbon,
  lace edging, silk flowers etc

**Preparation**

**1** If you are making boxes, draw the
diagram on white card and cut out. Score
along the broken lines, fold up the box
and tape the corners.

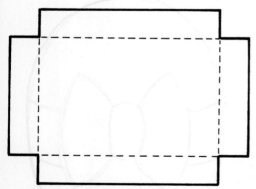

Draw this box tray pattern to any size desired.

**Working the design**

**2** Stand the box on the wrong side of the
giftwrap paper and draw round the base.
Turn the box on its side (still in the same
place) and mark the depth of the side on
the paper.

**3** Draw all four box sides onto the base
outline. Add ¼in (6mm) to the long edges.
Add ¼in (6mm) to the sides of the
corners.

**4** Cut out the shape. Snip into the
corners. Press folds into the paper along
the marked lines.

**5** Smooth out the paper shape. Spray
adhesive onto the wrong side. Stand the
card box on the paper and fold up the
sides, overlapping the corners for a
smooth finish. Turn the top edge to the
inside of the box.

**6** Cut pieces of edging from the doily
and stick them round the inside top edge
of the box, so that the frilly edge shows.

**Finishing and assembly**

**7** Cut a piece of stiff gift ribbon, crinkle
ribbon (untwisted) or cord for a handle.
Staple the ends to the long sides of the
box.

**8** Crumple a little tissue paper (or cut
tissue paper shreds) and put a layer at the
bottom of the box. Add small gifts,
sweets etc. Decorate with ribbons or
flowers as desired.

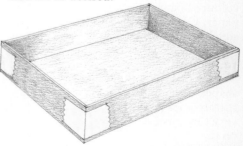

Tape up the corners.

# Candy cones

*For a really quick and easy table decoration, you cannot beat paper cones. These have been filled with delicious sweets but you can also use cones for dried flower holders.*

**Materials**
Patterned giftwrap, metallic giftwrap
Double-sided tape
Gift tie ribbons
Sequins, buttons

**Preparation**
1 Cut an 8in (20cm) square of giftwrap paper for each cone.

**Working the design**
2 Roll the paper from the bottom left corner to form a cone.

3 Fasten the overlap with double sided tape. Flatten the cone slightly so that the point is central. Turn up the other end and tape flat.

**4 Decorating the cones** Stick three buttons of different colours along the front of a pink cone. Stick four heart-shaped sequins along the front of a yellow cone. Make a ribbon rosette and stick it to a green metallic cone. Cut a piece of pink gift tie ribbon and cut the ends diagonally. Stick to a striped paper cone. Decorate with a tiny bow of pink ribbon.

5 Crumple a piece of soft tissue and push it into the cones to hold the shape.

6 Lay the cones on the table and fill them with sweets.

---

**Ribbon roses**
Although tiny ribbon roses can be purchased, you might like to try making your own for decorating candy cones and baskets. Cut a 6in (15cm) length of ½in (1cm)-wide gift ribbon. Working towards you, roll the right hand end into a tight tube (A). Hold the bottom of the tube in your right hand, very firmly. With your other hand, fold the ribbon away from you diagonally (B). Then roll the tube onto the diagonal fold and keep rolling until the ribbon lies straight again. Make another diagonal fold and roll the tube onto it (C). Keep doing this until all the ribbon length has been used up (D). Take the ribbon end under the rosette and catch it to the underside with a few stitches – or a touch of quick-drying glue.

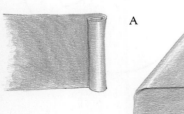 A 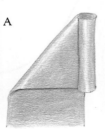 B 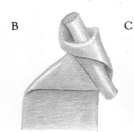 C  D

# Circus party theme

*Here's a sure winner for a children's party theme — circus clowns, paper flowers, balloons and multi-coloured streamers — and all the fun of the fair! Children can help with colouring in the clowns.*

## Materials
White paper table-cloth
Paper plates and beakers, without patterns
Heart-patterned ribbon, 1in (2.5cm) wide, 54in (135cm)
Double-sided tape
Coloured, non-toxic, felt-tipped pens
Stiff, white card
Red card
White cartridge paper
Gummed-back, coloured paper squares
Coloured pipe-cleaners

## Preparation
**1 Place setting** Spread the paper cloth on the table. Fasten down at intervals with thumb tacks (for safety).

**2** Position the paper plates round the table. Pencil round the plates. Remove the plates.

## Working the design
**3** Cut 2 15in (37.5cm) strips and 2 12in (30cm) strips of heart-patterned ribbon. Using the double-sided tape, tape the ribbons in a rectangle round the plate outline, to make the effect of a place mat.

**4 Clown plates** Trace the clown face features and transfer to the coloured sticky-backed paper. Stick the pieces to the plates (see picture).

**5** Cut the red hat from card and stick this on the rim of the plate. Decorate the hat with sticky-backed paper shapes.

**6 Clown beakers** Trace the clown figure and transfer to white paper. Colour the clowns with felt-tipped pens. Cut out and stick to the beaker sides.

**Trace this clown pattern for the beaker.**

### Clown cake
Make two chocolate sandwich cakes. Cut eyes, nose and mouth from one. Sandwich the cakes together with butter cream. Pipe butter cream round the eyes, nose and mouth. Pipe more cream into the eyes. Top each with a yellow chocolate bean. Place the cake on paper doyleys. Make a paper cone hat.

**6 Place cards** Trace the clown figure and 2 feet shapes. Transfer to pieces of white card. Colour the clowns with poster colours or felt-tipped pens. Cut out. Bend up the bottoms of the legs. Bend one leg back a little and one forward. Stick on the feet so that the clown stands up.

**7 Straw flowers** Trace and cut flower shapes from cartridge paper. Cut a circle for the middle of the flower and decorate with a sticky-backed paper shape. Tape the flower to the end of a pipe-cleaner. Wind the pipe-cleaner round a straw and stand it in the beaker.

Cut a flower shape from paper. Tape a pipe-cleaner to the back.

**Trace this clown pattern for the place card.**

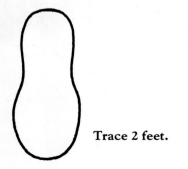

**Trace 2 feet.**

**Finishing and assembly**
**8** Place the plates on the mock place mats and stand a decorated cup to the left with a place card clown. Stand a decorated straw in each beaker.

**9** Wind paper streamers through the party table. Hang coloured balloons overhead with more streamers trailing from them. Sprinkle chocolate beans on the table-cloth.

74

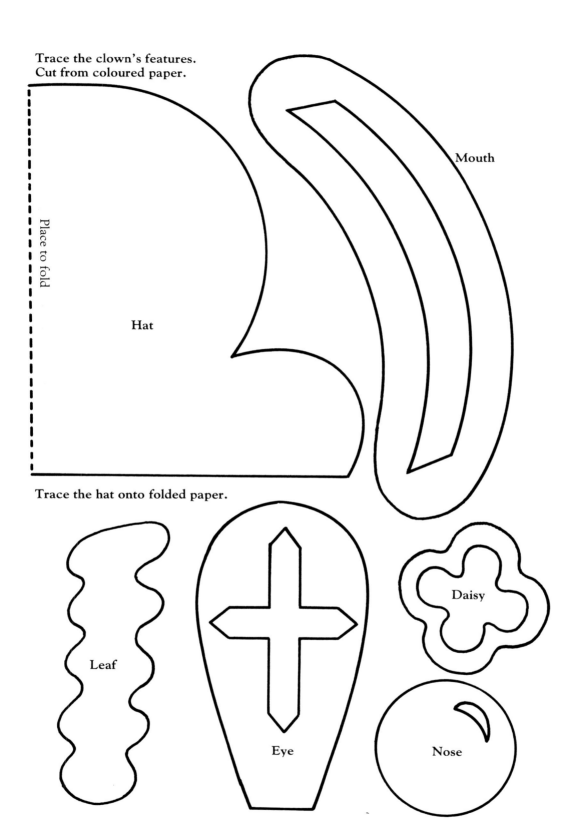

Trace the clown's features.
Cut from coloured paper.

Place to fold

Hat

Mouth

Trace the hat onto folded paper.

Leaf

Eye

Daisy

Nose

# Great outdoors

*A glittering stars mobile adds a touch of fantasy to a formal outdoor dinner party. Pale colours are used for after dark – or try sunny, warm colours for a daytime party.*

## Materials
(For a 6-place setting)
Squared pattern paper
Pale green or white cotton for a
    tablecloth Medium-weight card
Clear, quick-drying adhesive
Silver glitter dust
Silver cord

## Preparation
1 Work out the size of your table-cloth from the chart. Cut the fabric to size, joining pieces as required. Join pieces with run-and-fell seams, so that the cloth is neat on both sides.

2 Finish the cloth edges either with a narrow machine-stitched hem or with a single zigzag-stitched hem. Alternatively, you can stitch matching satin ribbon round a square or rectangular cloth.

Stick 2 pieces together with the length of cord in between.

3 Trace the stars and shooting stars patterns. Transfer the motifs to the card and cut out. You will need 2 shapes for each star.

## Working the design
4 **Stars** Stick 2 stars or 2 shooting stars together with a length of silver cord between them. Leave to dry then spread adhesive thinly on one side. Sprinkle thickly with glitter dust. Leave to dry.

5 Spread adhesive on the other side, sprinkle with glitter dust. Hang the decorations to dry. (They can be tied to a coat hanger.)

6 Tie the ribbon ends to a lampshade ring. Tie 3 hanging ribbons to the lampshade ring and suspend the mobile over the table.

## Finishing and assembly
7 Spread the cloth on the table. Fold the napkins decoratively. Place on the setting plate. For the table centre, arrange twisted candles – silver, green and white – of different heights in clear glass holders. If you like, the candles can be surrounded with fresh, white flowers.

8 Hang the glittery stars and moons over the table. Tie back bushes and shrubs, if necessary, with crinkle paper ribbon.

---

### Party stars
Laminate plain, striped and spotted giftwrap papers to card. Cut plain and patterned stars, stick two together over coloured threads.

---

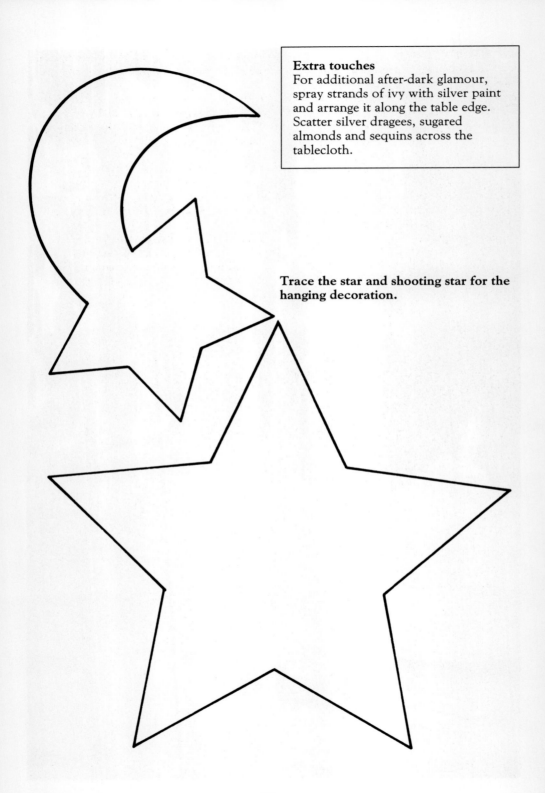

**Extra touches**
For additional after-dark glamour, spray strands of ivy with silver paint and arrange it along the table edge. Scatter silver dragees, sugared almonds and sequins across the tablecloth.

**Trace the star and shooting star for the hanging decoration.**

## SUNNY SETTING

For a daytime party, use warm, sunny colours for your patio table-cloth and napkins. The table-cloth can be finished at the edges by fraying back to a fringe or by sewing on a thick, cotton fringe.

1 Cut a rectangular or square cloth. Machine-stitch all round the raw edges, working 1in (2.5cm) from the edge. Clip into the cloth edges at 6in (15cm) intervals, almost up to the machine-stitching. Pull out the fabric threads, leaving a fringe.

2 If you are attaching a bought fringe, turn the hem to the right side of the fabric and press. Machine-stitch the fringe over the turned hem, working on the right side of the cloth.

3 Work 12in (30cm)-square napkins either with a fringed edge or by turning a single hem and zigzag machine-stitching the napkins all round.

4 For a centrepiece, stand a vase in a larger glass container. Fill the container with orange fruit. Arrange fresh flowers in complementary colours in the vase.

5 To complete the scheme, pieces of colour-matched crinkle paper ribbon can be tied in large, dramatic bows to nearby shrubbery.

# FOUR

# Christmas Festivities

# Mock pot for a tree

*Realistic-looking, artificial trees are ideal for small, centrally-heated rooms but the unattractive tri-foot needs to be hidden. Here's an idea for a mock pot that is simply made from card.*

## Materials
Stiff, good-quality, coloured card
Patterned gift paper
Gold, lurex ribbon, ¼in (6mm) wide

## Preparation
**1** Measure the width of the stand and the depth from just below the lowest branch to the table top. Cut 3 rectangles of card to these measurements.

**2** Measure carefully and punch holes down both edges of all three pieces of card. The holes must be exactly aligned on all the pieces.

**3** Thread the ribbon in a bodkin and, starting at the bottom, lace 2 pieces of card together, tying the ends in a bow at the top.

**4** Lace the third piece of card between them, to complete the mock pot.

## Christmas windmills
Cut 2in (5cm) squares of brightly coloured, shiny-surfaced paper, gold or silver foil paper, or you can laminate 2 sheets of giftwrap back to back.

Measure and mark the middle of the square. Cut from the corners to within 3mm (⅛in) of the middle. Take each corner to the middle and stick down with a touch of glue. Stick a tiny bead to the middle. Leave to dry, then stick a cocktail stick to the back of the windmill. For extra sparkle, you might spray the windmills with adhesive, then shake glitter dust over them.

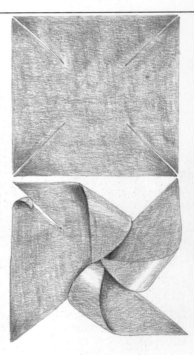

Lace the pieces of mock pot together with ribbon.

## Finishing and assembly

**5** Decorate the tree with small toys and games, foil-wrapped miniature parcels and decorations. Make small, coloured-paper windmills and add these to the decorations. Make them in bright, strong colours and metallic foil papers. Stand the mock pot round the base of the tree.

# Greeting card display

*Everyone has favourite ways of displaying greeting cards but a decorated board has the advantage that it becomes part of your Christmas decorations and will last from year to year.*

## Materials
Hardboard or plywood
Green felt
Narrow, red velvet ribbon
Gold and green glitter pipe-cleaners
Small Christmas baubles, foil-wrapped
  parcels

## Preparation
**1** Drill 2 holes in the middle of the top edge of the board for a hanger. Thread string through and knot the ends.

**2** Stretch the felt over the board and push pins into the sides to secure it. Take the excess over to the back and staple the edges to the board. Remove the pins.

**3** Using pins, mark all round the board at 3–4in (7.5–10cm)intervals.

## Working the design
**4** Staple lengths of red velvet ribbon across the board, between the pin marks, both ways, so that a diamond grid of ribbons is formed.

**5** Twist gold and green pipe-cleaners round the intersections.

**6** Stick lengths of gold ribbon along the top and bottom edges, taking the excess over to the back and stapling them down.

**7** Stick the baubles, small parcels, baskets etc down both sides of the board.

Staple ribbon across the board to make a diamond grid.

## Christmas ring
Cut a 24in (60cm) circle from a sheet of red or green card. Measure 6in (15cm) in from the edges and cut out the middle leaving a ring. Laminate a patterned giftwrap paper to the card. Cut a 20in (50cm) circle of card. Cover with paper. Cut out the middle to make a ring. Working on the wrong side of the smaller ring, spread a line of strong glue round the middle. Place it on the larger ring. Press down to fix it and leave to dry. Pierce 2 holes for a ribbon hanger. Use the ring for greenery or greeting cards.

# Children's decorations

*Children love to be involved in decorating the house for Christmas. Here are some simple ideas they can make by themselves. Small children may need help with cutting paper.*

**Materials**
Shiny-surfaced paper, metallic paper thin, coloured cartridge, good-quality giftwrap, crêpe paper
Clear adhesive tape
Stick adhesive
Adhesive-backed coloured shapes (optional)

## LANTERN
**Preparation**
1 Cut a 12 × 16in (30 × 40cm) piece of coloured paper. Cut a 10 × 16in (25 × 40cm) piece of metallic paper.

**Working the design**
2 Fold the coloured paper across the middle, cut slits from the fold to within 1in (2.5cm) of the edges.

3 Open up the paper, tape the metallic paper rectangle over the slits, along the edges, metallic side down.

4 Bring the short ends of the lantern together, overlap and tape. Cut a strip of paper $\frac{1}{2}$ × 4in (1 × 10cm). Stick the ends to the inside top edge of the lantern. **To display:** Thread the lanterns on a length of glittering or coloured cord, suspend across the room, along the wall or across the window.

## ZED STREAMER
**Preparation**
1 Cut 3in (7.5cm)-wide strips from the long sides of sheets of coloured tissue. Stick 3 (or more) strips together.

2 Concertina-fold the strips to 3in (7.5cm) wide. Press the wadge flat with the hand.

3 Make cuts into the wadge from the top and bottom edges, 1in (2.5cm) apart, with the outside cuts only $\frac{1}{2}$in (1cm) from the folded edges (see diagram). Open out the paper streamer. **To display:** thumb-tack or tape the streamer to the walls or across the window.

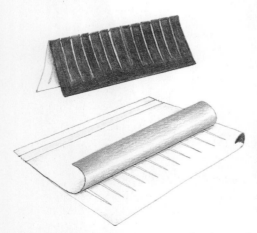

Lantern: Stick the foil paper over the slits on the wrong side.

Zed streamer: Cut the wadge like this.

86

## PAPER CHAINS

1 Cut pieces of damp-and-stick gift ribbons 6in (15cm) long. Fix the ends of a strip together. Slip the second strip through, stick the ends. Slip a third through, stick the ends. Continue until the chain is the desired length.

## LADDER STREAMER

1 You need 2 packets of crêpe paper in contrasting colours (such as red and green). Remove the crêpe paper from its wrapping. Cut through the folded edges from top to bottom on both sides.

2 Work with 1 piece of red paper and 1 piece of green paper. Stick red to green on the long edges.

3 Fold the red/green paper lengthways. Make cuts into both long edges, about 1in (2.5cm) apart, to form one ladder.

4 Work more ladders in the same way. Stick ladders together on the short edges. **To display:** thumb-tack or tape the streamer across the room.

Ladder streamer: Make cuts into both long edges.

## CONCERTINA CHAIN

1 Fix the ends of two contrasting damp-and-stick gift ribbons together at right angles.

2 Bring the left-hand strip up and fold over the right-hand strip. Bring the right-hand strip up and fold over the left. Continue, folding left over right, right over left to the end of the strips.

Concertina chain: Fold left hand strip over the right.

3 Stick the strip ends together, open up the streamer. **To display:** thumb-tack or tape the ends to walls or across the window. Made with metallic paper strips, this streamer is ideal for decorating the Christmas tree.

# Stars above

*This delicate looking mobile decoration will turn in air currents to shimmer and shine. It looks fantastic if hung where it reflects in a mirror, and doubles the effect.*

**Materials**
Tracing pattern paper
Card for templates
Silver crafts foil
Silver coloured card
Silver thread
Narrow silver ribbon

**Preparation**
1 Trace the half-star shape on folded paper. Transfer to cardboard. Cut out for a template.

2 Use the templates to cut 40 stars from foil and 40 from silver card.

3 Cut 8 lengths of thread, 50cm (20in) long.

**Working the design**
4 Stick a foil and a card star together, with the thread between them, about 8in (20cm) from the top end of each of the threads.

5 Leave a gap and stick on the next 2 stars and continue until there are 5 stars on each of the 8 threads.

6 Draw an eight-point star on silver card twice. To do this, draw a 7in (18.5cm) square then draw another on top. making a 45° turn. Pierce 8 equidistant holes round the edge of one card star.

7 Pass the ends of the eight silver threads through the edge holes and knot them on the wrong side of the star.

8 Stick the second card star on top, wrong sides together.

9 Pierce 2 holes in the centre of the large star and thread a length of silver ribbon through for a hanger.

**Trace the half-star shape on folded paper.**

Draw 2 squares, one on another.

Place to fold.

# Good enough to eat

*Winter branches make attractive table trees on which you can hang Christmas baubles, small gifts – or, as here, delicious marzipan fruits and sweets.*

## Materials
Branch from a shrub or tree
Quick-drying adhesive
White, matt, spray paint
Silver crafts enamel
Flower pot
Sand or gravel to weight the flower pot
White fabric or felt, 18in (45cm) square
White muslin
White dress net

## Preparation
**1** Trim dead leaves, weak stems, loose bark etc from the branch. If the shape is not tree-like, you can stick another, smaller branch into the middle fork.

**2** Spray-paint the branch white. Leave to dry. Brush silver paint onto the top side of the branches and down one side of the 'trunk'.

**3** Lay the flower pot on the edge of the wrong side of the fabric and roll it, marking the top edge with a pencil as you roll. Start again and mark the bottom edge as you roll the pot.

**4** Cut out the shape, adding 1in (2.5cm) top and bottom.

**5** Fit the fabric round the pot and overlap the back edges. Trim the excess away, so that the edges overlap about ½in (1cm). Stick the fabric round the pot, turning the excess at the top to the inside and at the bottom to the underside of the pot.

**6** Fill the pot with weight and stand the prepared branch in the filling.

### Sweet tree
You can develop the idea of an all-sweet tree. Petit fours and small, home-made biscuits, jewelled with fruits and nuts are ideal. Chocolates wrapped in foil, toffees wrapped in clear, coloured film, and fruit jellies strung on thread will make garlands. Liqueur chocolates are usually in foil and are attractively shaped. Foil-wrapped chocolate money is often presented in gold net bags. You could also wrap foil-covered chocolate eggs in circles of gold net.

### Dressing tree and pot
**7** Thread sweets and marzipan fruits on silver thread or wire and hang them from the branches. Drape muslin through the branches decoratively. Fold and drape muslin round the top and bottom edges of the pot. Crumple net and arrange on the top surface to cover the filling.

### Marzipan fruits
Colour white marzipan with liquid food colouring. **Strawberries:** shape red marzipan, mark seeds with a toothpick, make a stalk from angelica. **Bananas:** shape yellow marzipan, brush brown streaks with coffee essence. **Oranges:** Roll balls of orange marzipan, press against a grater for peel effect, use cloves for stalks. **Apples and pears:** shape fruit from pale green marzipan. Brush apples with diluted red food colouring. Use cloves for stalks.

# Fireplace arrangement

*This elegant display is made from pine-cones and nuts, with shiny red apples for colour. It is designed for a fireplace but would look equally well displayed on a table.*

**Materials**
Large bowl or dish (such as a soufflé dish)
   with kitchen weights in the bottom
Chicken wire netting, about ½yd (45cm)
Florists' tape
Sphagnum moss
12 large pine-cones, 8 smaller pine-cones
Nuts, five different kinds such as cobnuts,
   chestnuts, walnuts, almonds, Brazil
   nuts
Wood adhesive
Florists' stub wires
Sprigs of greenery, such as blue pine,
   holly, variegated holly, spruce (or
   other greenery)
Red apples, polished

**Preparation**
**1** Scrunch the chicken wire into a ball so that it fits into the weighted dish. Fix the wire in place with strips of tape. Cover the wire with sphagnum moss.

**Working the design**
**2** Stick clusters of nuts together, keeping to the same kind in a cluster. Leave to dry.

**3** Make wire stems for the nut clusters, twisting the wire between the nuts, then twisting the ends together.

**4** Wire sprigs of foliage to make stems.

**Finishing and assembly**
**5** Insert the large cones into the edges of the dish. Add the smaller cones, then insert the nut clusters. Insert sprigs of foliage, then finally arrange the apples.

Stick clusters of nuts together, twist wire through the nuts for a stem.

Twist wire round greenery sprigs to make stems.

# Christmas candle ring

*Based on the traditional advent wreath, this centrepiece is simple to make and uses seasonal greenery. You can adapt the design to a door wreath, if you prefer.*

**Materials**
Florists' block ring, 9in (22.5cm) in
    diameter
Florists' tape
Cake board
Plastic candle holders
Candles, four 9in (22.5cm) long
Florists' stub wires
Satin (or gift) ribbons
Seasonal foliage, ivy, holly, blue pine
    sprigs etc
Dried teazle heads
Artificial holly sprigs

**Preparation**
1 Tape the ring to the cake board. Insert the candle holders, spacing them equidistantly.

**Working the design**
2 Push foliage sprigs into the ring, to cover the outside and inside edges of the ring.

3 Add sprigs of berries, teazle heads and more foliage.

4 Cut 4in (10cm) lengths of ribbon. Fold the ends to the middle and twist a piece of wire round to secure the bow. Twist the wire ends to make a stem. Push the wired bows into the arrangement.

**Finishing and assembly**
5 Wire the candle ends. Insert the candles into the candle holders.

**Festive wreaths**
Buy a foam ring or make the wreath base yourself with wired greenery. Then decorate. **Berries and herbs:** Wire aromatic herbs and sprigs of berries together. Intersperse with wired dried roses. Add gold ribbons.

Holly and ivy: Twist fresh ivy with gold-sprayed ivy, add red ribbons. **Grapes and greenery:** Make a wreath from plaited raffia. Wire in small bunches of green and purple grapes, add vine leaves or sprigs of other green leaves. Add purple ribbons.

# TABLE-CLOTHS AND NAPKINS

Few people have all the table linens they need for a big party – and usually resort to using a bed-sheet to cover the table! Party table-cloths are not difficult to make and can be stored away for future occasions. Polyester/cotton sheeting, which comes in wide widths and in a range of pastel shades and strong, fashionable colours, as well as patterns and prints, is the favourite fabric.

## Measuring for fabric
### Square and rectangular cloths

Measure the length and width of the table top and add 9–12in (22.5 × 30cm) on each side for the overhang. If you are going to have a plain, machine-stitched hem, add 2in (5cm) on each side.

If you have difficulty in obtaining wide sheeting, or want to use a fabric other than sheeting for your table-cloth it will be necessary to join pieces of fabric to obtain the width. Obviously, a seam down the middle would look ugly. The ideal way is to join widths of fabric to the long sides of the main piece. This works very well if the joins can be on the table edge or part of the overlap. If the fabric is narrower than the table top you risk the seam being where the plates rest so it is better to cut the main piece even narrower and have the seam about 10in 25cm) from the table edge. You may be able to use the cut-away fabric to make table napkins.

**Joining panels of fabric** Cut the table-cloth panels with an extra ½in (1cm) on each side. A plain seam can be used but for good-looking table linens which last, use a run-and-fell seam.

To work this, machine-stitch with the wrong sides of the fabric together. Press the seam open. Trim one side's seam allowance by ¼in (6mm). Press the other seam allowance over it and turn and press under ⅛in (3mm). Baste and then machine-stitch through all the thicknesses.

## Making hems

Mitred corners look best on table-cloths. Press under ¼in (6mm). Fold and press the corner up. Trim the corner off diagonally leaving a hem allowance. Press the hem. Fold in and press the sides. Slipstitch the mitred corner.

## Bound edges

Bias binding, bought or hand-made from the fabric itself, is a neat way of finishing a raw edge – and can add a touch of colour or pattern to a plain fabric. Bias binding can be purchased in plain colours and patterned cotton.

If you are making your own, first cut bias strips from the fabric. Fold one corner to meet the cut edge. The diagonal

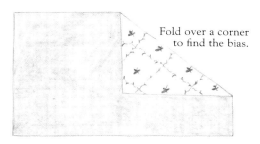

Fold over a corner to find the bias.

Cut the main piece narrower and have the seam about 10in (25cm) from the edge.

## Flowers for party tables

Float camellias in water in a glass cake stand.

Half-fill a sundae glass with water. Trim the stem of a full-blown rose and put it into the glass. Set one before each guest.

Fill small whisky tumblers with florists' glass nuggets. Fill the glasses with water. Insert 3 large flowers in each glass. Arrange the glasses down the centre of a long table.

For a table centrepiece, balance glass containers – cake stands, stemmed champagne glasses and sundae dishes – one on another to make a balanced shape. Fill the containers with water, position flower heads and trailing foliage to form a cascade.

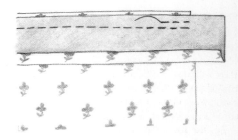

Baste, then stitch, the binding along the seam line.

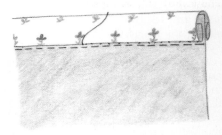

Fold the binding over, slipstitch in place.

fold is the bias of the fabric. Measure strips of the desired width from the diagonal edge.

Measure strips from the diagonal cut edge.

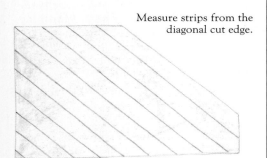

To bind an edge, lay one edge of the binding against the fabric, right sides facing. Pin and baste. Machine-stitch, taking a ½in (1cm) seam. Trim the fabric edge a little. Fold the binding over to the wrong side. Baste, then slipstitch in place, working over the previous stitches.

## Foliage in arrangements

If you are looking for ways to economise with party flowers, use leaves of different colours and shapes with just a few, good flower heads.

**Angelica** These leaves are a good, lime green.
**Dogwood** This has striped green and white leaves.
**Decorative kale and cabbage** These have green, white and red foliage.
**Elaegnus pungens** These are lime, green and yellow.
**Hostas** have many varieties that provide leaves in a range of shades from yellow to green and striped grey-green.
**Pieris formaosa** This shrub has greenish-white 'lily of the valley'-shaped flowers.
**Eryngium and eucalyptus** have grey foliages.

## ROUND CLOTHS

A round table-cloth is most easily cut from a square of fabric and, if you are using sheeting, there are no problems. All you have to do is measure the table top, add the overhang, 9 – 12in (22.5–30cm) and cut out the circle of fabric. To do this fold a sheet of paper in quarters.

Make sure the edges are level. Take a long piece of string and get someone to hold the end at the middle-of-the-paper corner. Hold the other end with a piece of chalk. Pull the string so that it lies

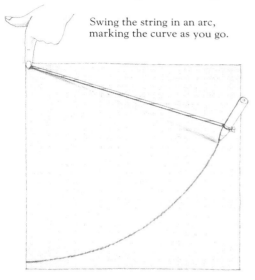

Swing the string in an arc, marking the curve as you go.

along the adjacent edge and on the corner. Make a mark. Now swing the chalk and string to the other corner, making marks in a curve as you go.

Cut out an pin the pattern to fabric folded in quarters. Cut out through all the layers.

**Adding fabric width** If you have to join on extra fabric, add side panels as you did for the rectangular or square cloth.

### Finishing hems

The easiest way to finish the hem of a round table-cloth is with bias binding. However, if you prefer a hem, try this method. Cut the round table-cloth with an extra 2in (5cm) all round. Fold the circle of fabric in four and spread it on the floor. Pin all the layers together. Using the string and chalk again, measure and mark the middle of the curved edge. Insert straight lines of pins from this mark to the folded edges. Cut through all layers of fabric. The cloth is now an octagonal shape, with straight edges which you can finish with an ordinary hem or with applied strips of fabric.

## NAPKINS

If you are making these yourself, you can afford to make them a good size. The best size is 16 – 18in (40 – 45cm) square but you can make lunch napkins slightly smaller 14 – 16in (35 – 40cm).

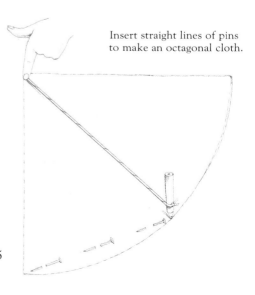

Insert straight lines of pins to make an octagonal cloth.

Pin the paper pattern to folded fabric and cut out.

## DECORATIVE TABLE LINEN
### Stencilling

For original and personalized party table-linens, stencilling is ideal. There are many ready-made stencil designs available from art and crafts shops, and several stencil pattern books are available. The designs are traced from the book page, transferred onto stencil blanks and then cut out.

Stencils can be used with fabric paints and a stencilling brush or fabric painting pens. (Stencilling brushes have short, stubby heads with the hairs squared off.) The techniques involved are simple and straightforward.

### Cutting your own stencils

Trace the design on tracing paper. Transfer the design to a stencil blank (which is a thick piece of waxed paper). Use ordinary typist's carbon paper for transferring. Work on a cutting board or a piece of thick cardboard. With a sharp scalpel knife, cut very carefully along the marked lines, cutting towards you Cut away only the areas of the design which will be painted, leaving the parts in between.

### Working with a stencil

Stencilling can be used to decorate many surfaces besides paper and cardboard – walls, ceilings, woodwork, doors, furniture, small furnishing accessories of glass, wood, paper etc and, of course, fabric. Special paints are available for different types of surfaces. Fabric paint and fabric painting pens are used for stencilling fabric. The colour ranges of fabric paints are vast – and silver, gold and bronze metallic paints are also available. These latter colours are ideal for decorating table linens for parties.

Wash the fabric to remove any dressing and iron smoothly. Spread the fabric on a flat working surface, on several sheets of newspaper.

Dilute the fabric paint as instructed by the manufacturer, but keep it fairly thick. Put a little in a saucer.

Position the stencil on the fabric.

Secure it at the edges with small pieces of tape, unless you feel confident about holding the stencil firmly with your hand. Dab the stencil brush in the thick paint, dab of the excess on scrap fabric, then proceed to dab paint in the holes of the stencil. Begin in the middle of the hole and then work out towards the edges. Do not be tempted to re-load the brush with paint while working an area (unless it is very large) or you may risk excess paint seeping under the edges of the stencil. You should aim for an even spread of colour, without patches or very wet areas.

Lift the stencil from the fabric very carefully and clean it with a dampened paper towel. Position the stencil for the next motif.

If the motifs are close together, let the one you have just painted dry, and work in another part of the fabric.

Similarly, if you are stencilling in more than one colour, the first colour must be completely dry before attempting to work the second over it.

### Finishing

When all the stencilling has been completed, the fabric is treated to make the paint permanent. Some fabric paints are pressed to make them permanent. With other types, the painted fabric is washed and then ironed. Finish in the manner the paint manufacturer recommends.

---

### Wired candles

To ensure that candles can be lifted from candle holders easily, wire the ends like this. Cut 3in (7.5cm) lengths of stub wires and hold them round the candle end, with the wire ends protruding underneath. Bend the ends under the candle and bind them all together with wire. Insert the wired candle into the candle holder.

## WORKING WITH PAPER AND CARD

### Tools and equipment

Many of the projects you will undertake in making decorations involve paper and card of different kinds. Most of the equipment you need is readily available, and you may have most of it already.

Your work surface is important. This should be at a good working height, flat and stable. You will require a protective surface to use over the work top, to protect it from cuts and scratches when using knives. A sheet of thick card or board is a suitable protection but should be replaced frequently as the surface will become pitted with cuts.

### Cutting tools

You will need two kinds of craft knives: a heavy duty knife, like a Stanley knife or an X-acto knife, for cutting thick card, and a small knife, preferably a scalpel, for thin card and paper. You should always cut straight lines by lining up the knife against a firm, straight edge. Use a metal rule for this rather than a plastic or wood ruler, as these materials can easily catch in the blade.

You will need several pairs of sharp scissors. Have a pair of small, easy-to-handle scissors with straight, pointed blades for most cutting jobs, a longer broad-bladed pair for general cutting and manicure scissors for cutting out intricate shapes.

It also helps to have one or two drawing aids – a pair of compasses, a set square, a ruler with small measurement markings, paper clips and a stapler. You will also need a pencil sharpener and a selection of hard and soft pencils. Carbon paper is useful for transferring designs.

### Paints

When working with paper and card, colouring in is sometimes necessary. You can use poster colours, acrylics, water-colours or felt-tipped pens.

Varnish is used for protecting work and this can be gloss, satin or matt finish.

---

Beads and glittering stones can be put onto salt dough decorations. Press the beads into the dough before baking so that there is an indentation. After baking, painting and varnishing, stick the beads into the indentations.

---

Use a varnish suitable for paper. A spray fixative can be used to protect finished work. This leaves a protective sheen on the paper, making it less likely to mark or stain.

### Adhesives

Clear, quick-drying and non-trailing craft glue is a good multi-purpose adhesive for paper and card. Use a glue-spreader for an even coverage. Stick adhesives are suitable for some paper projects. They come in a roll-up tubes and are clean and easy to use. Spray adhesive is useful for large areas but tends to be a bit messy for small pieces of paper.

### Laminating

This technique is used quite a lot in paper crafts. In laminating, the surface of card or paper is sprayed with adhesive, then a thinner paper is applied to the surface.

---

### Colour fun

If coloured candles are not available, dip ordinary, white candles in coloured wax for a three-coloured effect. Melt wax granules in a double boiler (or in an old saucepan). Add candle wax dye. Dip one end of the candles in the melted wax. Hold it in the air for a few seconds and dip again. Dip into cold water. Stand on the undipped end in a jar until the wax has hardened. Melt wax and colour for the other end and dip in the same way.

## PAPER AND CARD

In paper crafts, there are all kinds of papers you can work with. Artist's cover paper and rougher-textured Canson paper are available in a good colour range and they cut, crease and curl well. Cartridge or construction paper is now available in different qualities and comes in a few colours.

Tissue papers are available in a wide colour range and the better qualities are surprisingly strong.

Crêpe paper, also easily available, comes in a range of colours, in both single and double thicknesses. The double thickness quality can sometimes be obtained in a two-tone effect and is ideal for making paper flowers.

Giftwrap paper is enormously valuable in paper crafts. The better qualities fold and crease well, and some of them have metallic finishes.

Another popular craft paper is paper ribbon. This is presented wound tightly in coils, so the ribbon has to be gently unfurled to the required width. It is ideal for making ties and bows and for plaiting and weaving.

### Card

Artist's mounting card is mostly used for paper crafts projects. It cuts and folds easily and can be used for making boxes and containers. Thin card – so thin it is almost thick paper – is sometimes available with a glossy surface. This is ideal for making place cards and invitation cards.

---

### Seasonal flowers

Very often, only two types of flower with foliage will make an attractive table arrangement. Here are some seasonal ideas:

**Spring:** Violets and primroses
**Summer:** Roses and gypsophila
**Autumn:** Pompon dahlias, two types and colours
**Winter:** Red carnations, berries and evergreen foliage

---

## CUTTING PAPER AND CARD

To cut round curves, mark the shape lightly with the knife point and cut round making sure the free hand is firmly pressing on the card to keep it from moving. To cut straight lines, line a straight metal edge against the line to be cut. Press the craft knife firmly against the metal edge and draw the knife towards you, keeping an even pressure. To score card, cut lightly, just enough to break the surface of the card.

---

### REMOVING GLUES

Adhesive manufacturers will always help with advice about solvents for their products and some will supply these solvents direct if you write to them. In general, the first step in glue first aid is to scrape off any deposit and then proceed as follows:

**Clear adhesive**
On skin, wash first then remove any residue with nail varnish remover. On clothing or furnishings, hold a pad of absorbent rag on the underside, dab with non-oily nail varnish remover on the right side.

**Adhesive tape residue**
White spirit or cellulose thinners may do it. Or try nail varnish remover. Adhesives vary and you will have to experiment.

**Latex adhesive**
Lift off as much as possible before the adhesive hardens. Keep the glue soft with cold water and rub gently with a cloth. Treat any stains with liquid dry cleaner. Scrape off any deposits with a pencil eraser.

---

## RIBBONS AND BOWS

Decorative bows can be used in almost every kind of decoration. This bow is especially for flower arrangements. The water-resistant ribbon obtainable from florists is the easiest to work with but polyester satin ribbon can also be used. Form a length of ribbon into a figure-of-eight, holding the centre between thumb and forefinger. With the same length of ribbon make another figure-of-eight, holding the bows together at the centre. Bind the two bows together with a lightweight stub wire, leaving two mounting legs.

Bind the two bows together with wire.

Form the ribbon into a figure-of-eight.

Leave two wire legs for mounting.

Make another figure-of-eight.

### Crinkle paper bows

This is a particularly flamboyant bow and good for big displays of flowers. Untwist 3yd (2.75m) of paper ribbon rope. Make a small 2in (5cm) loop and bind tightly with reel wire. Make a second loop, slightly larger and bind again. Continue making loops of increasing size, binding each one tightly at the same position. Leave the last length of ribbon straight. Twist the reel wire ends together tightly leaving two legs.

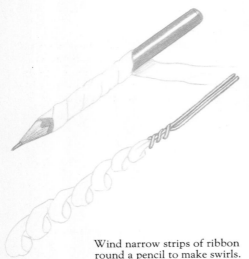

Wind narrow strips of ribbon round a pencil to make swirls.

## Daisy bow

This works best with cut-edge gift ribbon. Cut 4 pieces about 8in (20cm) long. Lay the pieces in a star shape. Stick at the centre with glue. Bring up the ends and glue together to make a ball. Dab glue inside and then push the top and bottom together firmly until they stick.

Daisy bow.

Swirls can be added by cutting narrow lengths of ribbon and wrapping the strips round a pencil. Pull out the pencil, attach a mounting wire and add the swirls to the centre of the bow.

## Rosette

Loop the ribbon as shown, tie in the middle with another piece of ribbon. Spread out the loops. Fish-tail the ribbon ends. This design can also be turned into a star by cutting the loops and fish-tailing the ends.

## Flat bow

Cut a strip of cut-edge ribbon and bring the ends together. Stick the ends to the middle with glue. Make a slightly smaller bow in the same way and stick on top of the first. Make a third, smaller bow and stick on top of the second. Cut a short strip of ribbon and bind round the three joined bows.

Flat bow.

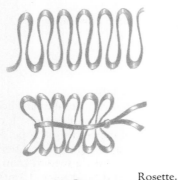

Rosette.

## Chrysanthemum bow

Cut ½in (1cm)-wide cut-edge ribbon into 16in (40cm) lengths. Stick the strip ends together to form circles. Twist the circles into figures-of-eight, dab glue to hold the shape. Join 2 figures-of-eight with glue.

Make more figures-of-eight and add them, laying them first one way, then the other until a chrysanthemum has been formed. You will need about 14 circles to get the effect.

## Painted china

Plain, white or solid colour china looks most effective in three-coloured party schemes. China can also be decorated with china paints for a special effect. Keep designs very simple – spots or lines around the edges. Painted plates can be used for most kinds of foods and can be hand-washed afterwards in warm water but the design will not survive a dishwasher.

## Tapes

Different kinds of adhesive tapes are used in crafts. It is recommended that you have three kinds of tape by you, transparent sticky tape, double-sided tape and masking tape.

Chrysanthemum bow.

## Party safety

Party decorations are very often made of materials that are flammable and so great care must be taken to see that accidents are minimised.

● Watch lighted candles carefully. Do not hang material near them which can catch alight. Keep any decorative material at their base low level and, to be safe, extinguish candles before they burn halfway down. Consider floating candles for decoration rather than those standing. Candles in water are obviously less of a fire hazard.

● When bringing decorative electric lights out of store for use, check the flex and electric plug very carefully. Check each bulb. Make sure that you are not overloading electric points with the additional lighting.

● Never trail lighting flex across the floor or allow it to hang across areas.

● If you find it necessary to extend the length of electric flex, have this professionally done – do not simply twist wire ends together.

● Make sure that the family first-aid box is well-stocked.

## Acknowledgements

The author thanks Jan Bridge, who made all the decorations and without whom this book would not have been possible. The publishers and the author would like to thank the following companies and organizations for supplying materials, photographic properties and information.

**Offray ribbons** supplied by Tootalcrafts Ltd, Units 1/2, Westpoint Enterprise Park, Clarence Avenue, Trafford Park, Manchester M17 1QS.

**S.P. Publishing**, Lower Tower Street, Birmingham, B19 3EN, for decorative wrapping papers.

**Henkel Chemicals** for adhesives.

**3M** for adhesives tapes.

**Paperchase**, 49 Pancras Road, London NW1 2QB, for Christmas decorations and decorative papers.

**Hedgerow Countryware Ltd**, Unit 18, Brent Mill Estate, South Brent, Devon, TQ10 9YT, for dried flowers and herbs.

**Candlemakers Supplies Ltd**, 28 Blythe Road, London W14 0HA, for candlemaking kit and information.

**Price's Patent Candle Co Ltd**, Solent House, 1258 London Road, Norbury, London SW16 4EE, for candles and candle holders.

**Manic Botanic**, 2 Silver Place, London, W1R 3LL, for plants used in photography.